Looking Inland

Looking Inland

Christine Evans

POETRY WALES PRESS
1983

POETRY WALES PRESS,
56 PARCAU AVENUE, BRIDGEND, MID GLAMORGAN

© Christine Evans, 1983

British Library Cataloguing in Publication Data

Evans, Christine
Looking inland
I. Title
821'.914   PR6055.V/

ISBN 0-907476-24-4

All rights reserved. No part of this publication may be reproduced, stored in a retrieval system, or transmitted in any form or by any means, electronic, mechanical, photocopying, recording or otherwise, without the prior permission of the author.

Cover Design: Cloud Nine Design

The publisher acknowledges the financial assistance of the Welsh Arts Council

TYPESET by AFAL, CARDIFF
PRINTED IN 11pt BASKERVILLE
by
**D. BROWN & SONS LTD.,
BRIDGEND, MID GLAMORGAN**

Contents

Bonanza 7
Callers 8
Funeral of a Grandfather 9
View from the Island 10
Part Timer 12
Summer in the Village 13
A Common Failing 14
Unseen Island 15
The Focus 16
Winter Visiting 17
First Spelling 19
Gatherers 20
Foghorn 22
Mynydd Rhiw 23
Travelling 24
Winter Digging 25
Ordinary Level 26
Weaning 27
On Video 28
A Gentler Salt 30
For a Spell 31
Summer Term 32
English Lesson 33
Exchange 34
Lesson 36
Idiom 37
Library in Autumn 39
First Lamb 40
The Sea 42
Labour 43
After the Bell 44
Neaps 45

Alert	47
Driving Home	48
Another Season	49
Solo	50
The Fisherman	52
Loss of a Shepherd	53
October Colours	55

Acknowledgements

Certain of these poems have previously appeared in *Anglo-Welsh Review*, *Poetry Wales* and *Stand*.

Bonanza

"Words," he told me, trying to be helpful,
"Respond through craft and concentrated effort.
A recluse alone can have the time
For the ceaseless innovation
And the hours of contemplation."

So that was the end of that.

Then, in between
Washing some nappies, preparing a lesson, kneading the bread
And lambing a speckle-faced ewe,
I stumbled over a poem; and now they spring up
Haphazard as mushrooms after August rain,
Glistening, and jostling
To be picked.

          But, after
Exhilaration comes
The business: I had not ever known
How hard it is
To throw discovery away.

Callers

It is always a shock when they take off their caps,
Those neighbouring farmers who call at our house.
They have to, of course, to have something to roll
Or to press or to twist in their blunt, nervous hands;
But it makes them instantly vulnerable
With their soft bald spots or thinning forelocks.
They seem at once smaller, and much more vivid:
Leaping out of type to personality.

The smell of their beasts comes in with them,
Faint as the breath of growing things in summer,
Rich, as the days draw in, with cake and hay and dung.
They are ill at ease in the house:
One feels they would like to stamp and snort,
Looking sideways, but have been trained out of it —
As with leaving mucky boots beside the door.

Only small, swarthy men with the friendly smell on them;
Yet walls press close and the room seems cluttered.
I am glad to go and make obligatory tea
As their voices sway, slow with the seasons,
And, ponderously, come to the point.

Funeral of a Grandfather

All over again, we bury our childhood,
Another eyelid's weighted down

between us and the hundred generations
he was part of: servant

of the seed, but a master of horses;
a sure steady drover; a striker

of twigs, ever hopeful of trees;
a seaman, a shepherd — a tender of detail.

On this windswept hill we stand apart a little
from the important public grieving

that perhaps he would have wanted —
he had such passion for the proper word

and the number, that ballooning magic
that eclipsed his world

and made us strangers. His heart
was wordless as a sheepdog's, shy,

like his hands indoors. Their roughness
snagged the baby's shawl. Accepting

the quiet corner of our lives, sometimes
we'd see him shake with silent laughter:

his eyes were warmest then. Their blue could be
as meek as flowers', enduring as the ocean.

With the strength of his forebearance
may our sons learn humanity, survive.

View from the Island

"Energy and terrorists." The words hang stark
Against the easy evening light, staying on
To meet the boys from mackerel fishing
Between a sea and sky so shining-still
The mainland seems suspended in mirage
And each man's voice a muted elegy.

"Inevitable shift to authoritarian regimes.
And isn't it the only way
To feed us all?" "Orwell, then?
Peace without justice, globally?"

A western shore, no harbour, just a welcoming
Of shingle in the rock, the tang of old bait
By a driftwood bench. Low water, and the little kids
Discovering new landscapes.
                                            "Conscription's
Bound to come . . ." "But catastrophes are rare.
Barbarianism moves
In great slow waves, technology
Will short across the gaps . . .
Rome's values still persist, remember."

Seaweed sometimes is pungent as a memory,
Smarting the eyes. And then the quiet one stirs,
Stemming the talk of rioting gangs, Jehad
And holocaust, pollution beyond salve:
"Yes — " drawing on his pipe, voice
Sure as the dusk that wraps us warm
And hides his eyes, "It seems the end,
One way or another, of our species.
What shall we say, a hundred thousand years?
Five thousand since the written word convinced us
We're masters of creation? Such ambitious
Primates — " "Spurious biology!" the insect man

Protests, waving his net
In agitation, while the History Prof
Smiles tolerantly and the rest of us
Gaze seawards. Brian from the lighthouse
Clears his throat, reaches for more beer.
"Not just sensational. I simply feel
The focus gone, we've run our course.
Adaptability and sharing, that made us
What we are. Now none of us
Will reach out towards change."

"Neurotic pessimism — " "There's a basking shark!
Anyone got glasses? Just see the size of him . . ."
But the long hand of Time that turned us up
And tilts the earth out from the setting sun,
Sucking the tide back in, dictates that I
Disturb the child who plays absorbed
Among the rockpools at the ocean's edge.
Bedtime. For Jane, the goats to milk; men's meals
Will draw the other women safe into routine.

Colours strike sharper just before they fade.
A dun mare drowses, foal against her flank,
And all around the hay is hushed and ready.
The men are gutting fish and joking now,
Raucous in this pause. "Who was that man
Who talked so much down there?
What did he say about the dinosaurs?"
"No-one. A man on holiday. Forget it.
The little owls are hunting, do you hear?"

But most clearly I remember walking home
In that short sweet hour before the dark —
A moment sealed in summer ignorance.

Part Timer

Yes, he says, he has
A few pots out from Porth.
Does not explain how from the earliest days
Out fishing with his father and an uncle
It was a refuge from the day's repeated toil:
A different dimension.

For one thing, no women,
With their nagging at his conscience, or his senses.
Only exhilaration and the early morning air
Rinsing the closeness of the cowpen from his clothes,
Stirring old sediment
Beneath the bother in his brain.

Now, like a drug,
It draws him more and more.
His eyes are always out beyond the islands,
Sharpening their blue with distance.
He leaves his cows hock-deep in dung
And lets the barley stand;
Fends off his wife to creep out in the dawn
And lingers on the beach
To come home with the tide.

The lobster cash
Is handy, he will say;
The visitors are always asking for a crab.
And — with diffidence — I don't mind
Going out, I like the fishing all right, too.

Summer in the Village

Now, you can see
where the widows live:
nettles grow tall and thistles seed
round old machinery.
Hayfields smooth under the scythe
simmer with tussocks;
the hedges begin to go,
and the bracken floods in.

Where the young folk have stayed on
gaudy crops of caravans
and tents erupt in the roadside fields;
Shell Gifts, Crab Sandwiches, To Let,
the signs solicit by the gates, left open
where the milk churns used to stand;
and the cash trickles in.

'For Sale' goes up again
on farms the townies bought with good intentions
and a copy of The Whole Earth Guide;
Samantha, Dominic and Willow play
among the geese and goats while parents in the pub
complain about Welsh education and the dole.
And a new asperity creeps in.

Now, you will see
the tidy management of second homes:
slightly startled, old skin stretched,
the cottages are made convenient.
There are boats with seats;
dogs with the work bred out of them
sit listlessly by garden chairs on Kodakcolor lawns;
and all that was community seeps out.

A Common Failing

Close-up of the shepherd's hands — hard,
Knuckles reddened in this first raw light;
Holding the ewe with spread and easy strength,
Then curving to a sinuous snake's head
To read the hot and sliding geometry inside her.

One small moist hoof uncurls into his palm.
There's another, hind leg, among the moss of wool.
Two heads, uncompromising domes of bone,
Float timelessly beneath his moulding fingers.
— A right old tangle we've got here. Now, steady.

Yellow as crocuses, heavy as wet rope,
The first lamb's hauled into the air,
Unfolded on the ground beside his mother's warmth.
Eyes shut indifferently, undemanding mouth.
— Now, lick him, damn it. Lick him into life!

No decisive head-shake. He's not breathing.
Concern, not technique, charges those hands now:
Chivvying, they rub and strike and pump
The flaccid chest, roll back an eyelid —
Are almost tremulous as the body heaves
To spend its one diminishing mew of breath.

For a moment, hang thumbs down.
— A good strong ram lamb, too. The other's small.
Warmth starts to seep from the congealing flesh;
All that deliberate, intricate growth, waiting
For ignition — if we only had the trick.

Now just degenerating chemistry, it's tossed
To rot with elder corpses on a casual bed
Of stale straw, dung, and half-burnt polythene.
Hands washed, the shepherd moves on up the hill.
Death's a common failing: his mission is survival.

Unseen Island

From across the sleeping sound
the unseen island
nudges at my consciousness —

wind-blown Enlli; nowhere
more steeped in calm,
more resonant of growing.

There, air trembles with associations
and I am played to a tune
I scarcely recognise

easy as water, but earthed.
Is it energy or faith
that breeds content in me?

Washed smooth, drawn out,
moulded to acceptance
like clay on a wheel,

so like a compass I am pointing
always where you lie —
elusive, shimmering —

but no mirage:
my unblurring.

The Focus

Reading Plath's letters, a minor revelation:
I no longer wanted to be dead.

She knew, none better, the clean bone of despair
Beckoning through the layers of litany —

Smothering, the reproachful ash of love
That can't accept the logic of release;

Pleasure sloughed off in raw and ragged flakes;
A child's security, a clear shell charred —

Now gleaming, easy, these flesh my days.
It seems, because I have begun to write.

For I tested, conjuring again
The gentle anonymity I once craved.

Resistance stirred, a corner fluttering
That swelled to purpose beating round my head —

From a few words? From finding the voice
That, surreptitious as a small brown bird,

Has crept under the eaves of my imagination
And built from its weavings of old syllables

A barricade at my back door, a focus
In the draughty barn that was my spirit.

And if anything comes of its nesting seems irrelevant:
For the wings of its protection are enough.

Winter Visiting

So, you are here again,
Your thoughts humming through me
Easy as water. Oh, yes, I agree,
It is not good
To be too long alone — here, sit with me,
If you can watch me
Paint this window; have my chair.
Let your bones soak up this winter sun.
February is the coldest month,
They say. To me, it's full of questions:
A month for the survivor.

     I know,
Your best were days like pumpkins,
Slow and golden.

See the cow out there, she looks
Drunk with sun. She stands
Considerate, rock-steady when I milk her.
Her winter coat is warm, black plush, her breath
A ghost of summer evenings.
I remember you walked home to Cambridge once
Through moonlit fields of sleeping cows
That made the night more tender.

My tabby cat distracts me
With her narrow, hunter's face, her vulnerable paws.
Her purring changes without warning
To a paranoid attack. She was
A stray; something's damaged her
For life.

How did it begin, this
Visiting of yours? I can't recall
Inviting you; in fact, I never liked you

Much — the adulation put me off, the fuss,
And then my mother telling me I should —
Until by chance (I thought) I came across
Your letters home, and, seeded by your zest,
My mind began to simmer with new memories.

Just jot this down for me, would you?
My fingers are all paint. No, I quite forgot:
You have no hands, of course, they're rotted through.
Somewhere I read the womb remains till last.
Wouldn't you guess it, dragging on
Like a smelly old doormat of a dog
Stubborn on the trail of the white bitch moon.

Glad you enjoyed that, I got it out specially.
Yes, I have babies, just the same as you,
And apple trees, and buried daffodils.
Unpredictable as joy, a robin comes
To take crumbs from my outstretched hand.
I thrive in quiet; am dull, botanical,
With a startled face like a refugee's.
There's nothing really here to interest you.

There's another big difference, too.
I am not mad like you.
Oh, no, I was never mad as you.

Now your thoughts begin to buzz
Angrily, avidly. I have no sweetness for them,
I must shake them out, your brilliance,
Your stings. No, no, no —
I cannot cope with you.
Back into the cold you go.

First Spelling

"Is there an 'i' in me?"
At four, he is too young to understand
That words, like selves, can sound quite different
According to their context. But in that moment
Kneeling on the mat with chalks and paper,
I seem to see a line of duplicated sons —
Each one an 'I' in his small being —
And pray that energy and purpose
Will merge their voices into one sweet tune.

Gatherers

They taste of the uplands,
bilberries do: of
rain through the heather,
peat thin-scarfed
over acid rock. A small darkness,
nudging identity,
like the smell of woodsmoke or the way
firelight flickers
on half-seen faces in November.
Eating them in winter from the deep freeze
resurrects the kindness
of that day we snatched
to go and look for them, climbing
out of sea-fog to discover
in its steep stone streets Tre'r Ceiri held
an ancient clearness still. Only summits showed
in an ocean of drowned centuries;
the real sea was fathoms-deep, forgotten.
It was a world for women —
details stood out, safe.
The sky was a daylong yawn
of content, the smells all warm
moist earth we were part of,
just women gatherers. A kestrel
hovered close, a brood of choughs
screamed at the wheeling blur
beneath their wings, and all
afternoon we talked, were quiet,
and picked, our ease absolved
by being useful. The children found
harebells and tormentil, got wet feet,
drowsed in white heather
beside some bones they thought a fox's kill.

"We must come again," we said,
but with no conviction, knowing
the three-fold pivots of our lives
would swing us out of range.

So, "That's the last of them,"
I say, "— this year's bilberries —"
but though the winter sea
bays at my back door, the wind
has ice on its breath,
that day's warmth, I have it still,
I've gathered it.

Foghorn

With bovine persistence
it shudders through the night
leaning close, or muffled
as it nuzzles comfort
in the cold, thick skirts
that have fallen round the islands;

every two minutes, a great
egocentric cry
and never any answer;
no need of one.

I know it is only a clever
contraption of wires and sensor cells.
Deliberately, recall relief
when, with compass on the blink
and fog swell feinting ever closer, pounding
on a shore where none should be,
we picked it up
to haul ourselves on course again.

But still, its sufficiency chills me
more than the clammy salt that seeps
under the door. They will go into eternity,
the machines, blaring our priorities
to a universe oblivious as fog —

switching on at twilight;
beaming down unlooked-for images
of the well-stocked silos
in Missouri and Okhotsk;
automatic muzzles lifting
(once in a hundred years)
at a fault on the radar screens;
until the sun itself
runs down; is blotted out.

Mynydd Rhiw

"Higher," Taid would urge,
Forking more loose hay up to a load
Precarious already. "Lots of room
Above, you'll never bang your head."

And now I see his point, though
Perching on this cairn feels much the same
Pressed close by an exhilarating blue
That, later, will be sharp with stars,

For the island where those hectic summers were
Is dwindled to a daffodil bulb
Half-buried by the dark — a world
Contained as the intensities of childhood.

From up here we see it all
As the hawk does or the fighter pilot
Swooping the undulations
To rehearse a kill; grief or joy or goodness

Absolving into pattern
That like a well-made poem, will seem
The only version. Just to be here
Shrinks us into where, not who, we are:

Out on a limb,
At the extremity of a digit,
Poised on a ridge in a fingernail —
We grow dizzy at the scale of things.

We must go down.
The small places that we fill
Are waiting. It is not easy for my kind
To be detached, to stand up high.

Travelling

First frost in my explorer's beard
focusses a dream: we are bivouacked

in a northern country glorious by day
with gold dust dancing in our sunlit breath —

a halcyon progress, busy, well-companioned,
so sleep comes easy as to played-out children

and I alone, jerked back to wakefulness
by a crackling log, an inward-falling in the fire,

realise we are ringed by night and ice,
and by God knows what wolves of time

that pace us through the miles of muffling trees.
The best we can is fashion signals to the sky

and hope that somehow they are understood;
that from somewhere, anywhere, help may come.

No sense to rouse the slumberers, oblivious,
rolled in their blankets by the fire they trust;

no sense in eking out the dwindling stocks
nor reckoning what we're likely to lose first.

Solace, now our context is made clear,
lies with tenderness increasing as we travel

and equanimity, to outstare pain.
Each morning we'll move seawards once again.

Winter Digging

Deep in the well of winter
even smell is submerged;
acquiescence seeps
and pools, dragging at
the apple trees so lately planted.

Hours of silence. I am an island
of purpose, chivvying the ocean.
But a raven croaks above me, a black
defiance in the sky; a curlew, close, unchains
his syllables like confident balloons

and the grazing ewes
of cumulus are stirred
miles high, docile to
momentousness I cannot feel.
This field I work in falls

ragged to the sea, so all afternoon I sense
unease in its upheaving dunes,
shifting at a far Atlantic breath;
and while I can, with every spade,
I turn another summer in my mind.

Ordinary Level

It is all settled:
He is to do book-keeping.
These examinations almost
A formality; five years of diligence
Following the footprints of suggestion
Have kept him straight and safe.

Paper One, Question One:
Gravely, remembering
The lessons, he considers
All the titles' implications, jots down
Headings. Picks up his pen
With purpose — oblivious
To the others' sighing, restless
As a lane of hawthorns in the sun
And light south wind of early summer —

And chooses winter on a fishing boat,
The 'Determined', driven hard
In the race for mackerel.
Their iridescence and the scream
Of herring-gull, gannets diving by the stern,
And the emptiness of an Atlantic dawn

Dazzle him to all the rest.
Page after page
Of luxury. The next day,
And the next,
He carries on, through Chemistry and Maths
And Commerce. And waking

As he used to, in the dark,
He finds he has been smiling
In his sleep.

Weaning

This absorbs me like a new baby.

Each day slides through a haze
of delight and triumph and anxiety
for I am tuned
to a frequency too high
for ordinary hearing: intent
lest any word should wake,
stirring in the close warm quiet
and creaking the unsuspected cradles
where they grow.

No-one else will ever know them
as I do, quite from inside out.
I love and hate them for the hold
they have, compelling me
to tend their slightest murmurings.
The fat of my life
is burnt up, suckling them. I am
all bone, charged with a magic current.
I have no time for love, or frying chops.

For a while, they let me
carry them about, hugged safe, but soon
clamour to be set down —
to stand on their own terms.
They are strong enough to belong to others,
but all that energy
leaks out of me, like blood; things
are no more than themselves again.
Except that in myself, each time,
there is a minor alteration.

It feels like growing.

On Video

The spent kelt
Waits. Upland waters lip,
And tantalise with cool brown fingers, but he
Hangs in abeyance. The ripe world's
Shed her load, been fertilised.
He awaits a deeper absolution.

This image on the screen
Frees another from the deeper reaches
I believed were done with:

The merciless bright arena
Of modern dying — starfish cluster
Of masked protagonists, clasp of glass
And steel, electronics
And bleached air. For one young man
Just letting go: for him, too,
The quicksilver had faded.

I see now that no net of love
Could have held him,
But blindly we strove
To land him and preserve him
In our dry, consistent air;
Lines taut on hooks of blood
And oxygen and drugs and prayer.

He was beyond our terms of nourishment.
The pucker at his temple stood out
Sharp. His body's only hurt,
A fall from his bike one Christmas.

A dead poet, glazed and stiff
And futile as the great stuffed fish
We saw together in a seafront bar
Once, gawping at its genesis
Through a dust-thick case —

Or this T.V. presenter, pious voice
Turned off, the easiest of relevances gone.

A Gentler Salt

Where she lies dying
is hot, bright sun
but here, on this peninsula,
for the whole week, we
are muffled in sea-fog.

Each morning we climb out of it
driving the fifty miles
through a jangle of June colours
and past the woods' and the sea's beckoning
to arrange ourselves
on hospital chairs and sit out the hours:
show that we, too, can endure;
our eyes hardening
like lizards', crazing at eternity.

The journey home is easy, almost reflex,
like speeding backwards down a telescope,
and going out of focus. For the fog
has all day waited for us, soberly.
We float our minds on it
like sleep. It bathes our eyes
with a gentler salt; and hour after hour
as we lie in the dark, apart,
the foghorn from the lighthouse on the island
is inconsolable. And I begin
to be afraid of sunlight's splinters.

For a Spell

The day appointed came
And went, but by that time, ignored,

Time had relaxed his stalking,
Strolled, yawning, from the shadows

To curl up at her feet, her purring creature,
Claws drawn in and rippling velvet stripes

Submissive to her stroking. Forever
And the moment clung, cohered, and held

That winter when she first forgot herself
Discovering the man she loved at last —

So ordinary, miraculous, that feeling
Was the only world she cared about,

Bruising with love and ripening
Like a pumpkin oozing slowly into sweetness,

Giving back summer. Content
Blurred her features like a baby's

To unspecific tenderness, but, muffling
Like snowfall, grew too much.

Wasn't there something
I meant to remember? Look what you
Made me forget!

And after, though she always tried,
Time never once let her get close.

Summer Term

Two things about teaching again:
The slowly-greening lanes
That rinse my eyes
Morning and evening,
Glistening with tenderness
Seven years have taught me, too;

And the moody trampling
Of resentment
Gathering momentum
In the schools.

Morning and evening
The bluebells stand.
Horse chestnut leaves
Shake out their shining wings.
I should not need this lesson:
Their kindness springs
Out of the struggle
Of last year's dead things.

English Lesson

They strip the centuries from me
With their eyes, these hostile women
And the boys in the desks at the back
Hunching over their sullenness
Whenever I look their way.
So, helpfulness becomes
A patronage. We are doing précis
From past papers. Not my idea,
The syllabus, I tell them, I cannot help
The system; but feel only
That I strut and harangue
Them, captive as if
Their names and liveries
Were owed to me, their passage
Still unpaid. And when one boy
Sighing, too hot, rubs at his neck,
I seem to see the chains
As if an enforced march
Through forest still continues;
And temper bares
A ruthless Saxon bitch
Lashing them with their ineptitude.
Backed up against the blackboard I recall
It's fear
That makes the she-wolf snarl.

Exchange

I am doing The Red Pony
With 3B. Despite their appetite
For murder, horror films
And modern cannibals, they
Are easily moved
By animals. Aloud, they wonder
About the first that shared our lives:
Dogs, they agree, and orphaned goats,
Suggests the girl whose mother keeps
The wholefood shop. But *"Cows,* Miss?"
They do not see have anything,
Save meat and milk, to give.
So I do not try to tell them

How with the first cow that we bought,
Old, scarred and belly-sagged
With breeding, for a time I found
An old affinity, a new
Exchange. She had rosettes like flowers
Hidden in her glossy hide;
Her throat was soft as catkins
In the sun. She stood
Hock-deep in meadowsweet
Sighing as I milked her;
On winter mornings, breathed its fragrance
Through the stone cowshed. I warmed my hands
On her blackness, my heart
With her trust.

It was February, before dawn, hard frost
Squeezing the land to silence
When we loaded her. The concrete
Glistened like black slate.
It took my voice,

My hand on her flank, to get her
Stumbling up the ramp.
"Well done, Missus!" And I stood back
Smiling, as the bolts went home.
Eighty pence per kilo
On the hook. She was barren,
Useless. But I am glad
It was too dark to see her eyes.

Lesson

From a high cold hill
And the house called Scout
Clear as a wren, my sister sang
Till the April day school claimed her.
She made no murmur as I stranded her
On those unforgiving steps, bayed
By the gibing throng. Ruthless
With adolescence, I never once
Looked back to wave;

And muted ever since, she lost her place
In the relentless chant of tables and the drone
Of information. You've been there
So you know, you were processed too,
Singing All Things Bright and Beautiful
To the rasp of the cane between the rows
Before the desert hours, grit in the brain,
And the scorn of teachers,
Arrogant and veiled as Bedouins.

It took twenty years
And a catastrophe
To give her back identity
And start her learning
To be happy.

Idiom

I learn a new idiom
In local Welsh: 'Gone to the corner',
They say of the old who sit
By the fire,
A lifetime's usefulness
Trembling from their hands;
And the family faces, watching

Like we did in bed
For the candle flame to flicker —
Light leaping
Like a dying cat,
In desperation, gulping darkness —
And I shrink from
Such a public humbling.

But at least they have
More than their own warmth
To live by, in a small, slow world
That ticks with memories. So,
"It was the year Llew led the singing,
And he's gone to the corner
Five years this November." Faces

Imperceptibly fall in; the eyes
Cloud over; we throw away
All they believed in, resent
Their hanging on, and still they have
A place for emptiness to fill.
A slow corrosion
We could envy, despite our regulations

Re housing, diet, privacy,
And routine medication;

Provision for a favourite channel
But to all the rest,
Kept numb. For when we're old
We can only count on rights
To cling to, only votes to give.

Library in Autumn

It might as well be forest,
These tall ranks of shelves, sunlight
Cool as spilled lemonade
Across the tables, air
Unrippled. Unease shuts
Round them as the heavy door
Closes on the din of changing lessons.

The order bothers them: intruders
From an arid, boiling plain, they'd like
To shatter it, disprove the mystery
Of the shelves where the words
Sit still and innocent
As apples. When we're done,
They'll give them to the fire
Or cauterise this place
With labels, archive it
On microfilm for experts: The Era
Of the Printed Word —
Six Hundred Years of Reading.

First Lamb

Limp and sodden as old rags, stained
Like rust with the delay, it's eased round
And unfolded out of all her warmth;
Airseal at nose and mouth
Ripped clear, and shaken
Into breathing. Now the ewe must lick him . . .
But she will only stare in horror
As the struggling flesh that,
Meshed in mucus, seems persistent
To be part of her again.

She has never been caught before, this one.
How she ran, preferring talons in her belly
To the unknown grip of hands.
She wheels and stamps
Though nothing but the north wind pens her —
And this stranded creature, mouth already
Seeking in the angle of determination
Like a daffodil's blind aiming at the sky.

The afterbirth, a pendulum of blood,
Swinging, startles her into stampede:
Each step back's a slow defeat

And when suddenly he pushes out
A trickling cry — thin as a bird out to sea —
Inexorably, she is wound in.
By nightfall, she has the hunch
Of habitual solicitude; he,
A living lustre, glimmering
Like rare moss against her steadiness
In a dry, committed sleep.
Her eyes are unflinching in the torchlight.

Her neck is stretched, her nostrils full of him,
And she has even found a new voice.

Envy her programming:
She has only to listen
To learn tenderness, to be right.

The Sea

Doesn't live up to
half what I've heard;
staggering along the beach
aimlessly, leaning on rocks

at the headland. It's winter:
no one else is about.
When he raises his head
from the pebbles, I approach.

Teetering, full of good humour,
he leers at me
with his one white-rimmed shining eye;
lurches nearer,
with a wheezy laugh
and a faceful of rotten breath.

A drunken old marauder,
reduced to feinting
at the torpid sand.

At least, his Vikings
cannot wryly witness
his dragging jadedly along
after his supercilious

windowshopping

bossy moon of a wife.

Labour

The village midwife schemes —
How to involve these fathers! They should
Share responsibility, get up at night,
Stand by and help their wives in labour,
Unfeeling brutes.

        Yet I have seen them sweat
As though they're loading hay
Before a thunderstorm; stand around
Dull as cattle in a pen
Or retreated into corner chairs, heads down,
Their strong square hands, so capable
At turning lambs or helping cows to calve,
Fidgeting with caps or rolling
Continuous cigarettes.
The waiting room is acrid
With uncertainty: nervous as a bunch of colts
They wheel to face the Sister at the door.

The hard-liners — Can't see the point
In hanging round all day — have gone on home,
But find they cannot settle to a job.
Do a bit of fencing, check the sheep routinely;
Net a lobster pot or two, but all the while
Wonder what finality the phone will bring;
What new meaning's pushing to the light
In them.

After the Bell

Time becomes tacky, amber
As this slow, thick
Afternoon sun, and we are caught, we three
Invigilators, as the school goes home.

There is an old smell of feet. This gym
Is a canyon, we are using up
Its air. Alone with ourselves
And sixty-nine drowned faces
Carried slowly past us
Towards unguessed-at overfalls.

I calculate the smooth brown walls
To the window-rim, imagine clutching freedom
Scaling ropes and wall-bars; viewing round.
Outside grows lush with possibilities.

There is one peep-hole. Casually, in turn,
We each patrol and stand to look:
Remote and purposeful as sandpipers
In their trim white shirts, two fourth-year girls
Go by on passage to their real world

And that's all. The whispering pens
Are desultory now as breaths of wind
That lift and stir the ash
Of old volcanoes. We sink down and submit —

And there's the trick. Let
The moment simply be, and it is over.
Our voices boom out in the sudden clearness,
Hearty with instructions.

Neaps

(Neap tides are the smallest, i.e., when the sea retreats least.)

Walking the sands at low water
One autumn afternoon, the shining stretches
Flood her mind with new significance:

For fifteen years, she's been the shore
Swept clean; has lain like this
Reflecting only him
For the sky's examination.
Yes, tenderness they'd shared,
The thrumming wave, and winters wrapped
In his warm arms — but she had been
Smoothed-out with gratitude, while he
Had never really spoken, never
Undermined himself with words.
Even her screaming rage was swamped
In the monstrous incoherence of his thunder.

At last, she thinks, she'll turn inland,
Seek the small dry strips of privacy
Beneath the cliffs; is there still time
For scaling them, to face
Whatever ice or firing waits
To ring her round?

She drives her resolution home in front of her.

But the yard is silent, cowshed
And barn empty; earthy-heavy boots
By the back door, and sandwiches she'd left
Untouched. Brittle with fever, feeble
As the washed-out sheets, he hunches
In their bed with 'flu. Now,

For the first time, she notices
The white hairs flown at jawbone and at temple;
Like a blundered word.

The years run down like rivers at her back.
Her cliffs already crumble.

Alert

I am driving home as slowly as I can.
It is nearly night, November.
Light is draining up into the sky
Leaving a sediment of slow, white mist
To wind about the feet of waiting cattle
And fill the tunnels of the woods to wading.

Trees loom, massive and benign,
Over the road. It is their stark, ink-black
Strokes that have slowed me down.
They make signs
Against the sky, meaning in a script
I can almost understand.

Their trunks are concentrations
Of dark energy, dragged
From the earth; standing firm.
This was more than seeing.
I think of turning round and driving through
The wood again, but it might have changed

Or I would have changed; so crawl on
Under this insistent sky, keeping to the hedges.
Now windows are squares of warmth
But the only life my headlights catch
Is a white owl swooping, silent, for the kill.
Such stillness, such steeling: the season's question

Hanging fire.

Driving Home

Of all skies, winter's
Are most generous.
Mornings, my aim
Is for the sun — before noon,
Anything is possible.
But I am drawn back home

Effortlessly, by the day's last light
Glistening like the inside of a shell.
Behind me, all the hills of Gwynedd
Drown, their knuckles showing white.
Ahead, the swooping road that races darkness
Down this one last finger to the sea.

Up from the valley where the great trees
Are still gathering, near enough
To reach across for reassurance, as though
They smell the acid rain already,
There is no foreground: only
The scribbled silhouettes of hedges

Against the unfreckled foxglove of the sky.
Even telegraph poles take on dignity,
Lining the route. On the horizon, houses
Are blocked in, solid, cold
As Stonehenge until I'm past; then windows'
Shift and glitter makes me think of tinsel.

By the time the road unwinds and climbs again
I have headlights on, disturbing owls,
For the sharp new moon above the island
Is a token only and the pinks have hardened
To a cliff of jasper, staring out
The dark. Promising ice, but promising stars.

Another Season

Today we turned the rams out
On the mountain. Deliberate
As rainclouds with the purpose
Of next spring, they surged away,
Wheeling and quartering the ground,
A far-off flare jerking heads
To attention, putting fire
In stolid hooves.

By afternoon, they have homed in.
Fourteen ewes, I count, have been marked
Of those I can see; they flaunt
Their fertility, jigging
Red-painted rumps through the bracken —
A signal to set imagination leaping
The winter — five months
Of silent running.

They say we are in for
Fifty years of hard winters, a little Ice Age.
In this corner it is still so warm
A butterfly is opening like a flower
On the rock. Oh Time, lay down
Our children gently; keep them dry
As kindling, sure and innocent
As coal.

And still, russet coats fading, heather
Like bruises on their flanks,
These hills at the gates of Llŷn are lifting
Blind muzzles to the sea
That once they stalked: waiting
Against all hope
For their ancient Irish masters
To come home.

Solo
("Between Here And Now")

By this time the only other sound
is the slow drip of time
from the stone earth, wrung
scientifically in the hands of God —
himself at bay
in a random universe,
or the call of a bird
unseen, on passage, and speaking
of a green April
it is too late to share.

There is a window: but here, within,
waves' and lips' beckoning
is silent, flowers are dumb.
From its own emptiness
sunlight smiles and drools
over the bare rock
as he knows it has done
for six million years.

In this arid enclosed air
the spores of kindness
cannot grow
to eat at resolution; the apple
withers on its sweetness.
The only eyes he meets
are varnished over. Soon
even memory
will be walled up.

His hands are stained
with autumn but he will not
let them tremble or reach
out. His words

sink down to us
almost casually in the windless air,
settling
resolute as the last slow soundings
of a deaf man's concerto.

The Fisherman

Land speaks to him
Out beyond the islands:
You belong to me.

As he grows older, its beckoning
Becomes insistent. Walking the shore
For his nets, the wet sand blue
And scudding white with winter sky,
He leaves no prints. And yet
The gravestones at his back
Are the black wicks
Of his identity; the names on them
Outstare the tide. Hearing
The wind howl, its open mouth
Pressed against the window where he sits
To weld his lobster pots
Or coiling ropes, he's sure
His feet demand the firm horizons.
One more season; then the farm
Can home him and enfold him,
Warm with certainties.

Only, the sea longs
To lick
And lick him smooth.
His boat is turned
For harbour, but all day, inland,
He tastes the salt
That tightens on his mouth.

Loss of a Shepherd

for John Jones,
11th December 1982.

Dying on the mountain,
he would have had
the bracken's banked-up fires
to curl beside; the heather
that endures
where nothing else can;

ear still rounding on
the song of a wren at sundown
and wind's clearness, though the brain
could not record them,
nor the blue
his eyes outstared.

Badger and fox, the circling raven even,
could not have been more cold,
the December night far kinder
than the place she had to leave him in.

Two hundred miles, fourteen
dark hours away,
the sweater she'd just knitted
was rolled round warmth
his body could not hold.

Now, they will gather
to pile earth and words like stones
over his wholeness. But something
more than memory
survives, to keep the cold
from hearts in winter:

like the dogs for whom
his voice defined the world
and gave it purpose, you
who loved him have absorbed
his eagerness, his essence.

When new lambs stagger through the wet
or gleam like catkins
in March sun, remember most
he cared. And so, would not have wanted
to be looked for; to become a grief.

October Colours

We drove inland a hundred miles
and back today, through wet October colours —
scree slithering
cold and slow as metal
down the mountains; bracken's rust;
and in the passes, great black boulders
that waited for the ice
to pick them up again.

Then downward, speeding through a world
of falling brightness, where the eye
slipped smoothly round new bareness. An elm
black with dying snagged at the sky
like a broken tooth; and in a field
below the road, the roadworks and the lights on red,
I watched as we waited
a single oak tree feeling for the sun
like a giant hand, its centuries-slow
opening made plain; and saw

I like the early autumn in my life:
the way disguise
has no more point, and yet my tracks
are lightly covered over. In middle age
we can afford
to give ourselves away, to spend
affection easily as leaves;
bank up the fires with silence
if we choose. Yes, children die
of hunger still — disease
eats in — the helpless everywhere
are terrorised. We have no gods
inside or out,

to make it all come right; but
if we let it, kindness grows,
and though rage and grief still shake
us, they will not destroy
our relevance: not now; not yet.

The ramparts of our peninsula
beckoned us back, really blue
in the twilight — so brief, apologetic even,
since we ended Summer Time.
Now night exaggerates
our speed, the small safe journey
we shut ourselves inside. I long
to be home, yet
with each exploring mile
I sense a lightening,
as if my heart
has been unclenching through the years
as surely as an acorn's fist.